Though antinomianism and legalism are, from one standpoint, opposite poles of error, there is theologically, and often in experience, a link between them: for both proceed on the same false assumption, that the one and only purpose of law-keeping is to gain righteousness with God. Thus the legalist goes about to establish his own righteousness, while the antinomian, rejoicing in the free gift of righteousness by faith, sees no reason to keep the law anymore.

J. I. Packer, *God's Words: Studies in Key Bible Themes*, p. 104

I formerly served as a professor at a conservative Christian college. Perhaps three-fourths of my students had been reared in evangelical homes and attended Bible-believing churches. I recall one day in an American history class when we were studying the New England Puritans. My students had read Edmund Morgan's *The Puritan Dilemma*, a delightful biography of John Winthrop that discusses the Massachusetts Bay Colony's founding in the early 1600s.

For those who think that starting a community from scratch must necessarily look like one of television's *Survivor* episodes, the Puritan story is amazing indeed. These godly men and women relocated to a barren wilderness, embarking upon a task they regarded as a holy experiment. While not endorsing everything that every Puritan said and did, I nonetheless explained to my students why I regard many of the Puritans as spiritual giants. J. I. Packer's right: we need the Puritans today because they display a spiritual maturity that is exceedingly rare. (Packer makes this case in his superb book *A Quest For Godliness: The Puritan Vision of the Christian Life*.)

But I could tell during our class discussion that despite Morgan's favorable biography of Winthrop, my students did not share my respect for the Puritans. In fact, my students were surprisingly suspicious of these Christians whom I regarded as my spiritual heroes. I asked my class, "Was there something wrong with the Puritans? You don't seem to like these people." After a long silence, one of my students spoke up. "Well, you know, the Puritans were . . . er . . . they were legalistic."

I asked, "They were legalistic?" He answered, "Yeah, they were legalistic." I asked the entire class, "Do you all agree with that? How many of you think that the Puritans were legalistic?" Almost every hand went up.

On the chalkboard, I wrote in big letters the word *legalistic*. Then I asked my class, "Would someone please define that word for me?" Silence. "Just get us started with a definition," I coaxed. "What is part of this word's meaning?" No response.

I continued. "How many of you have ever used the word *legalism* before?" All hands went up. I asked, "How many of you think the Puritans were legalistic?" Most hands went up again (although a little less confidently this time). "Can't you tell me what this word means?" Finally, one student haltingly said, "Well, they were just like, um, so concerned with obeying God all the time."

As he spoke, you could tell he realized this wasn't a good definition.

I asked my class, "Isn't it good to obey God all the time? What's wrong with obedience?" Nobody said a word. I asked again, "Can't anyone give me a biblical definition of this word?" Finally one of my students spoke up. "I think you've convinced us that we really don't know what the word *legalism* means."

Let me tell you about those students. Although this was a conservative Christian college, they rarely used the word *justification*, and they even more rarely used the words *regeneration* and *sanctification*. But my students could deploy the word *legalism* with the ease and confidence that comes with frequent use.

Since that day, numerous conversations have persuaded me that those students were not unusual. *Legalism* is a word that we Christians throw around with reckless abandon. It seems like every churchgoer can use the word *legalistic* with

Are You Legalistic?

Grace, Obedience, and Antinomianism

by Robert G. Spinney

Are You Legalistic? Grace, Obedience,
and Antinomianism
ISBN 0-9776680-7-X

1st Edition

TULIP BOOKS
P.O. Box 481
Hartsville, TN 37074 USA
www.tulipbooks.com

zest. Yet when I ask Christians to define the concept, I invariably get mumbled and imprecise answers. If you asked ten Christians to define *legalism*, you would likely receive ten different definitions.

Common Misuses of the Word *Legalism*

Here are some unbiblical uses of the word *legalism*.

We see a believer applying the Bible to a real-life situation. He's careful to obey God's commands, even God's seemingly little instructions. He's serious about his Christian life, perhaps more serious than we are. This brother has convictions or practices that seem odd to us (which often only means *not like our convictions or practices*). We don't say it publicly, but we think, "He's way too serious about obeying God. He should lighten up." And we look at that brother and think, "He's legalistic."

We see Christians discussing the meaning of a Bible instruction, like the Ten Commandment's "remember the sabbath day, to keep it holy." The discussion makes us uneasy, largely because we are unsure how to implement such a command today. Instead of joining our brothers and contributing to the difficult task of applying God's Word to our life, we dismiss the issue as unworthy of our time. We think, "I don't even want to consider how to obey that commandment. Obeying that command in any way today would make me look weird. I don't want to be legalistic."

We are having a discussion with a brother in Christ, and he suggests that we reexamine our ethical behavior in some area. We ask our friend for the biblical warrant for making such reforms, and he points us to a passage in the Old Testament. We respond by saying, "Oh, but I am a New Testament Christian. Jesus fulfilled the law, so I don't have to obey any part of it. All Old Testament laws are abolished." We walk away thinking our brother who values the Old Testament is legalistic.

A friend encourages us to apply God's Word to a seemingly small issue. He may suggest that we make financial restitution for a sin we committed years ago. He may suggest that our clothing is immodest. He may suggest that we should be more faithful in attending the church's Wednesday night prayer meeting. This strikes us as being too picky, an unnecessarily conscientious application of Bible teaching. We regard this careful (we would say overly careful) faithfulness as legalism.

In a local church, pastors do what the Apostle Paul did: they call upon the flock to fulfill biblical duties. These godly elders reprove, rebuke, correct, and exhort. They are even willing to say, "That particular unbiblical behavior will not be tolerated here. God's people must obey God's Word." Church members criticize such church leaders as legalistic.

A local church attempts to conform itself to the Word of God. In order to do so, the church establishes biblical standards of conduct. Maybe they write these biblical guidelines into their church's constitution and expect church members to honor them. But for some, the very appearance of rules and standards (regardless of how scriptural they are) provokes anger. They complain about legalistic church rules.

All of these uses of the word *legalism* demonstrate common misunderstandings of this concept. The unfortunate thing is that there *is* something called *legalism*. It is alive and well in the Christian world today; in fact, many of God's people are being wounded and burdened by genuine legalism. However, we rarely recognize it. Real legalism flourishes right under our noses—undetected—while we wrongly call obeying God's commandments legalistic.

Antinomianism and an Unbiblical Understanding of Legalism

In John 14:15, the Lord Jesus Christ says, "If you love Me, you will keep My commandments." Jesus is not reluctant to talk about commandments, is He? He's not afraid of being called a legalist. Indeed, Jesus says that the only real evidence that someone loves Him is obedience to His commands.

In the next chapter of John's gospel, Jesus says practically the same thing. John 15:10-11 reads, "If you keep My commandments, you will abide in My love; just as I have kept My Father's commandments and abide in His love. These things I have spoken to you so that My joy may be in you, and that your joy may be made full." The Lord Jesus Christ clearly affirms the necessity of obeying God's commandments. Some think that obeying God's laws is a joy-killer and is at odds with loving God, but Jesus did not think so. He saw no conflict between joy and obedience or between love and obedience.

Jesus' disciples reiterated their Master's message. Consider 1 John 2:3-6: "By this we know that we have come to know Him, if we keep His commandments. The one who says, 'I have come to know Him,' and does not keep His commandments, is a liar, and the truth is not in him; but whoever keeps His word, in him the love of God has truly been perfected. By this we know that we are in Him: the one who says he abides in Him ought himself to walk in the same manner as He walked." Keeping God's commandments is not optional; obeying God's laws is not something regrettable called legalism. According to this passage, the person who claims to be a Christian but habitually disobeys God's commandments is not a Christian at all.

What was Jesus' attitude toward God's commands? Consider Psalm 40:8, which the Holy Spirit attributes (in Hebrews 10:5-9) to the Messiah. This is what Jesus said of Himself: "I delight to do Your will, O my God; Your Law is within my heart." Jesus did not say, "I run away from Your Law. It is a burden. I don't like it." No— God's Son said that He *delighted* to do God's will, a will that was expressed in God's laws.

As we consider this concept of *legalism,* we need to ask some questions.

A. Is it legalistic to obey God's commands?

Of course not! Surely all Christians must agree that obeying God is good and disobeying Him is bad. God saves people so they will obey Jesus Christ (1 Peter 1:2). The inspired apostle rejoiced over the Roman Christians' obedience (Romans 6:17-18, 16:19) and censured those in Thessalonica who would not obey God's instructions (2 Thessalonians 3:14). John 3:36 contrasts "believing in the Son" with "not obeying the Son." (See especially the NASB and ESV rendering of this verse.) The Bible praises Caleb because he "followed the Lord God of Israel fully" (Joshua 14:14); it doesn't condemn Caleb for legalism.

If we imply (as some do) that obeying God's commandments is legalism, then we also imply that God is the world's greatest promoter of legalism. This is because God has given men many laws and expects obedience to them.

This expectation did not go away when Jesus Christ inaugurated the New Covenant. Indeed, one key Old Testament prophecy declares that New Covenant obedience will be even greater than Old Covenant obedience. Jeremiah 31:31-34 says:

> "Behold, days are coming," declares the Lord, "when I will make a new covenant with the house of Israel and with the house of Judah, not like the covenant which I made with their fathers in the day I took them by the hand to bring them out of the land of Egypt, My covenant which they broke, although I was a husband to them," declares the Lord. "But this is the covenant which I will make with the house of Israel after those days," declares the Lord, "I will put my law within them and on their heart I will write it; and I will be their God, and they shall be My people. They will not teach again, each man his neighbor and each man his brother, saying, 'Know the Lord,' for they will all know Me, from the least of them to the greatest of them," declares the Lord, "for I will forgive their iniquity, and their sin I will remember no more."

God's implanting of His laws within His people and writing those laws upon their hearts is reiterated in Ezekiel 36:25-27:

> Then I will sprinkle clean water on you, and you will be clean; I will cleanse you from all your filthiness and from all your idols. Moreover, I will give you a new heart and put a new spirit within you; and I will

> remove the heart of stone from your flesh and give you a heart of flesh. I will put My Spirit within you and cause you to walk in My statutes, and you will be careful to observe My ordinances.

Note two salient features of the New Covenant, the covenant ushered in and ratified by the Messiah. First, God's commandments will be internalized within God's people. The Holy Spirit regenerates the sinner and works within his soul so that he understands and loves God's precepts. Second, the Holy Spirit empowers the believer so that he finds new resources to obey God's commandments cheerfully.

This is why Jesus can say that the essential characteristic of a true child of God is that he obeys God's will (Matthew 7:21). By the same token, the essential characteristic of a non-Christian is that he habitually disobeys God's laws (1 John 3:4-10). Law-keeping is a distinguishing mark of the Christian; law-breaking is a sign of unbelief.

Similarly, the Bible characterizes Christian holiness as the fulfillment of the Law's requirements. Romans 8:1-4 says that the crucified and risen Christ condemns sin's power in the believer and the Holy Spirit empowers the saint for holy living. The result? "That the requirement of the Law might be fulfilled in us, who do not walk according to the flesh but according to the Spirit" (v. 4). Law-keeping is worked in us by Christ's Spirit; law-keeping is not denigrated as unspiritual legalism.

Obedience to God's laws is good! That's why God puts His laws in our hearts and in our minds— so we will obey them.

Whatever we may think *legalism* is, portraying obedience to God as negative is simply not an option for anyone who embraces the Bible as God's Word. If the word *legalism* is in your theological vocabulary, be sure your vocabulary contains the word *antinomianism* as well. Antinomianism literally means *against law* or *anti-lawism*: it rejects the binding authority of God's moral instructions in the Christian's life. The antinomian is "so mesmerized by grace as to lose sight of the law as a rule of life." (Packer, *God's Words: Studies of Key Bible Themes,* p. 104) Bible-believers simply can't be antinomians.

B. Is it legalistic to be careful about obeying God's commands? Is it legalistic when we commit to obeying even seemingly small commands?

What does God say in Ezekiel 36:27? "I will put My Spirit within you and cause you to walk in My statutes, and you will be careful to observe My ordinances." God Himself makes us "careful obeyers" by the power of His Spirit.

In addition, we all know someone who obeyed even the smallest of God's laws, and I suspect we have never called Him a legalist.

Didn't the Lord Jesus Christ obey God's laws perfectly? For thirty-three years, Jesus obeyed God's laws perfectly, carefully, and minutely . . . not just in outward action but inwardly on the level of attitudes. As a toddler, the Messiah obeyed God's laws when He never threw a temper tantrum. As a small boy, Jesus obeyed God's laws when He loved the bullies who hurt him. As a teenager, the Son of God obeyed God's laws when He always maintained pure thoughts. As a young man, Christ obeyed God's laws when He interacted kindly with men for whom He labored as a carpenter. The logic of salvation demands that the Messiah obeyed *every* law of God— even allegedly small ones, never sinning, always doing what God required.

If obeying God's laws carefully and precisely is legalism, then Jesus was the world's greatest legalist.

Jesus' perfect obedience to God's commandments has ethical implications for believers today. Christians are commanded to live in the same manner that Jesus lived (1 John 2:5-6). We are to follow in Jesus' steps, which means regarding Christ as our example (1 Peter 2:21). Christians are to be conformed to the image of Christ (Romans 8:29), who was the greatest law-keeper who ever lived on earth.

C. Is it legalistic to obey God's commands too much?

I trust that simply stating the issue like this will expose its error. You can't obey God too much! And yet this sentiment is often lurking behind our unbiblical use of the word *legalism*.

D. Does obeying God's commands create joyless legalism? Will obedience to God's commands rob a Christian of his joy?

Satan's oldest strategy is to convince people that true joy lies in doing what God has forbidden and not doing what He has commanded. Consequently, the devil deceives us into thinking that God's commands are joy-killing straitjackets. Untold misery has resulted from the widespread belief that disobeying God promotes joy. A critical part of the Christian's progressive sanctification is the progressive unlearning of this lie through the renewal of our minds by God's Word.

So what does God tell us about the relationship between joy and obedience?

The uniform testimony of God's people throughout history has been one of joy in God's commandments. The psalmist said, "I have inherited Your testimonies forever, for they are the joy of my heart" (Psalm 119:111) and "The precepts of the Lord are right, rejoicing the heart" (Psalm 19:8). The apostle Paul echoes this sentiment when he says, "I joyfully concur with the law of God in the inner man." (Romans 7:22) In John 15:10-11, we see the Lord Jesus Christ speaking of obedience and joy in the same breath. He told His disciples, "If you keep My commandments, you will abide in My love; just as I have kept My Father's commandments and abide in His love. These things I have spoken to you so that My joy may be in you, and that your joy may be made full." What was Jesus' joy? What brought Him happiness? According to Psalm 40:8 (which Hebrews 10:5-9 attributes to Christ), Jesus thought like this: "I delight to do Your will, O my God; Your Law is within My heart." Jesus' joy was in obeying His Father, and He wants *this* kind of joy to be in us also.

How did the Lord Jesus Christ live while on earth? Nobody ever obeyed God the way Jesus did. He became obedient to the point of death, even death on a cross (Philippians 2:8). What was it that motivated Jesus to obey God even when it hurt so badly and cost so much? Hebrews 12:2 reports that it was "for the joy set before Him" that Jesus endured the cross. Unlike the first Adam, the second Adam rejected the lie that true joy lies in doing what God has forbidden and not doing what He has commanded. He looked through the pain and saw God in whose presence is fullness of joy and at whose right hand are pleasures forever (Psalm 16:11).

With both feet planted firmly on the ground of Christ's finished work at Calvary and by the enabling power of the Holy Spirit, we can and must do likewise. Pursued in this manner, God's commandments will not be burdensome (1 John 5:3). The joy of the Lord will be our strength (Nehemiah 8:10).

E. Is it legalistic to obey the moral laws found in the Old Testament?

Moral laws are ethical instructions aimed at our behavior, behavior that encompasses both external conduct and internal attitudes. The Ten Commandments are the foremost example of Old Testament moral laws. Is it legalistic to obey them?

Of course not. All laws—whether human or divine—are expressions of the lawgiver's character. The motive behind a law is always the lawmaker's desire. The same is true for God's laws: they are expressions of God's will. God's ethical instructions are shaped by His own moral character and His desire that men mirror His holiness (Leviticus 11:44, 1 Peter 1:14-16). It is critical to realize, then, that God has not changed: He has neither improved nor deteriorated (Malachi 3:6). Since the character of God has not changed (and God's moral laws are expressions of His character), moral laws that God proclaimed in 1300 BC are just as valid as moral laws He articulated in 30 AD. Neither God nor His ethical standards have changed; indeed, neither *can* change. This is why the Apostle Paul could write, "The Law is holy, and the commandment is holy and righteous and good." (Romans 7:12)

Consider the Lord Jesus Christ's words in Matthew 5:17-19 and how this passage affirms the perpetual validity of God's moral laws. Jesus says,

> Do not think that I came to abolish the Law or the Prophets; I did not come to abolish but to fulfill. For truly I say to you, until heaven and earth pass away,

> not the smallest letter or stroke shall pass from the Law, until all is accomplished. Whoever then annuls one of the least of these commandments, and teaches others to do the same, shall be called least in the kingdom of heaven; but whoever keeps and teaches them, he shall be called great in the kingdom of heaven.

However we wish to define the word *fulfill* in this passage, it surely does not mean *abolish*. The Messiah did *not* come to abolish what was declared in the Old Testament. Note also the word *annuls* in this passage, which means to loosen the force of something or to render something not binding. Jesus specifically said that He did *not* come to annul Old Testament laws.

Do you want to be called great in the kingdom of heaven? Then know even the least of God's commandments, obey them, and teach them to others. And a recipe for being least in the kingdom of heaven? Annul some of God's moral laws by saying that they are not in full force.

F. Do we sometimes use the word *legalism* to excuse our sin?

Lurking behind many misuses of the word *legalism* is a sad spiritual reality: The very core of sin is lawlessness (1 John 3:4), so we don't want to obey God. As fallen men, we have an aversion to law-keeping. This is one of the ways that we are just like our great, great, great, great grandfather Adam. As long as the remnants of sin persist in us (which will be until the believer is glorified), we will be tempted to disobey God. Antinomianism appeals to our flesh.

But we are churchgoers, and we know that we can't say, "I'm not going to obey God's laws." So, at least at times, we justify our disobedience with the word *legalism*. We escape the righteous demands of God's law by saying, "Let's not be too picky about obeying God's commands. Let's not talk about obeying rules. After all, we don't want to be legalistic." We use the word *legalism* to create a theological smoke screen. We use a word to strip God's laws of their binding power. This is little more than creating camouflage for antinomianism and sinning.

In these cases, the real issue is not *legalism* at all; rather, it is our unwillingness to repent of sin and obey Christ.

If these things do not constitute *legalism*, then what does?

A Biblical Understanding of Legalism

A. What is Legalism?

Legalism is an attitude (or motive) that leads people to try to establish, maintain, or improve a righteous standing before God by their own activities. Legalism is founded upon the belief that the Lord Jesus Christ's justifying and saving work must be supplemented by one's own works. It results in an unbiblical emphasis upon works in one's relationship with God, especially by injecting works into the matter of justification.

Notice here that legalism is not the deed itself, but rather the motive behind the deed. For example, giving money to God's work can be a legalistic action or a God-pleasing act of worship. The difference? The giver's motive.

A legalistic attitude assumes that what Jesus Christ has secured for His people is insufficient. The legalist says that he must do some things to supplement what Christ has done and thereby improve his legal standing before God. The legalist believes he has his part to play in bringing down God's grace to himself: when the legalist has done those things, he thinks he has become more acceptable to God. He thinks that he has earned more of God's favor. By virtue of his performance, he has secured something in addition to what Christ has secured.

Thus legalism is in some ways the opposite of antinomianism. Whereas antinomianism denies the validity and binding authority of God's laws, legalism exalts law-keeping above both God's grace and Christ's provision.

In order to understand legalism, it is important to realize that it is linked to the concept of justification. Justification is God's declaration that a man is legally just (or righteous) because all of the Law's claims regarding him are satisfied. How can a sinner—a chronic lawbreaker—be declared perfect before the Law? Because the sinner's sin is imputed to the Lord Jesus Christ (which results in pardon) and Christ's perfect obedience is credited to the sinner (which results in his being righteous before God). The justified sinner now stands before God as legally approved: his sins have been put to Christ's account and Christ's righteousness has been put to his.

Legalism vandalizes this key doctrine of *justification by faith alone through grace alone in Christ alone*. It is likely that the very word *legalism* was invented in the mid-1600s to express a perversion of justification. Our first documented use of the word is found in the 1645 writings of the Puritan Edward Fisher: he wrote that a legalist is "one who bringeth the Law into the case of Justification." (Remember the students in my American history class who thought the Puritans were legalistic? They were stunned to learn this little fact.)

Since legalism is a corruption of justification by faith alone, we need to consider briefly the doctrine of justification. We'll then return to consider legalism.

B. What is Justification?

Romans 5:19 reads, "For as through the one man's disobedience the many were made sinners, even so through the obedience of the One the many will be made righteous." Here is the doctrine of justification (indeed, the gospel itself) in a sentence. This verse states that Adam's sin is regarded by God as the sin of the entire human race. In other words, Adam's sin was imputed to (or put to the account of) all humans. The Puritans expressed this concept famously in their children's primer: *In Adam's fall, we sinned all.* This point—that the guilt of Adam's sin is assigned to all humans—is reiterated throughout Romans 5:12-21:

> by the transgression of the one the many died . . . the judgment arose from one transgression resulting in condemnation . . . by the transgression of the one, death reigned through the one . . . through one transgression there resulted condemnation to all men . . .

These verses express a concept that is called *the federal headship of Adam*. Adam was the representative head of the entire human race. Because a spiritual solidarity exists between Adam and all mankind, God regards Adam's sin as the sin of all mankind. Thus Adam's sin makes every human a guilty sinner from birth; Adam's guilt is imputed to every man. This means that (among other things) our status as sinners was guaranteed by Adam's sin in the Garden of Eden.

Federal headship is what makes salvation through Jesus Christ possible. In the same way that Adam was the federal head of the human race, so Christ is the federal head of a new race of redeemed men, namely those men who belong to God's family. Thus the Bible calls Jesus *the second Man* and *the last Adam* (1 Corinthians 15:42-49). Adam was the "first man" and the head of the entire fallen human race, but Jesus is the "second Man" and the Head of a new justified race. Just as Adam's sin was imputed to all men, so Christ's righteousness is imputed to all who repent and believe the gospel. Just as Adam's sin was put to the account of all whom Adam represents, so Christ's righteousness is put to the account of all whom He represents.

Romans 5:12-21 makes explicit the parallel between Adam and Christ. Consider verse 19: "For as through the one man's disobedience the many were made sinners, even so through the obedience of the One the many will be made righteous." Here are similar statements from this passage that present Jesus as the analog to Adam:

> Adam, who is a type of Him who was to come . . . the grace of God and the gift by the grace of the one Man, Jesus Christ, abound to the many. . . those who receive the abundance of grace and of the gift of righteousness will reign in life through the One, Jesus Christ . . . through one act of righteousness there resulted justification of life to all men . . . grace would reign through righteousness to eternal life through Jesus Christ our Lord . . .

Through the Lord Jesus Christ's obedience, many sinners will be declared righteous. Jesus' obedience was twofold. First,

He was obedient to God's laws throughout His entire earthly life. That means He earned a perfect righteousness— the only man on earth ever to do so (although Jesus was actually a God-Man who was both fully God and fully human). Second, He was obedient to the point of death, even to death on the cross. There the Lamb of God became a sacrifice to pay for sins. As a result of this twofold obedience, Christ earned a perfect righteousness, one that was then put to the account of God's people. It was imputed to them, just as their sins were imputed to (or put to the account of) the Lord Jesus.

This means that the justified sinner is both forgiven of all his sins (because they are imputed to Christ) and clothed with the flawless righteousness of Christ Himself (because it is imputed to the believer). The justified man stands before God with the same legal standing as Jesus Christ Himself.

It is critical that we appreciate the implication of justification: *the justified man cannot be any more righteous on the lawbooks of Heaven than he is at the moment of his salvation.* The newest Christian who has been justified by grace through faith in Christ is—at the moment he first believes—as righteous as he can ever become. That's because at the moment of his salvation, Christ's own righteousness is put to his account. The Christian will never be able to add to that perfect righteousness. To be sure, he will grow in sanctification: he will put to death the remnants of sin in him and more fully conform his life to God's Word. This lifelong process culminates in glorification. But with regard to his legal standing before God, *a justified sinner can't become more righteous than he already is.* There is no condemnation for those who are in Christ Jesus (Romans 8:1).

Martin Luther coined a beautiful phrase for this: he called it our *alien righteousness.* It is a righteousness that Another has earned, a righteousness that is outside of us and distinct from our own behavior. It is this alien righteousness put to our account that allows us to stand before God as justified people.

This is the heart of the Christian message. Luther rightly said that the church stands or falls on the doctrine of justification by faith alone.

C. What Does Justification Have to Do With Legalism?

Recall our definition of legalism: *Legalism is an attitude (or motive) that leads people to try to establish, maintain, or improve a righteous standing before God by their own activities.*

Legalism is built upon an unbiblical assumption, namely that the imputed righteousness the believer possesses in Christ is not sufficient to enable him to stand before God. Legalism says, "I need to supplement Christ's imputed righteousness with my own righteousness— with a righteousness constructed (at least in part) by my own good behavior." It also wrongly assumes that God owes us something for doing the good works that He created us to do (Ephesians 2:10) or for doing the self-invented "good works" that we think deserve reward.

The gospel declares, "The sinner is declared legally righteous before God based upon the imputed righteousness of Christ." Legalism declares, "The sinner makes himself righteous before God by his obedience to God's laws."

The gospel declares, "The sinner is justified by faith alone." Legalism declares, "The sinner is justified in part by his own works. Jesus makes it possible for the sinner to be righteous, and He may supply a good deal of the sinner's righteousness. But in the final analysis, the sinner's own contributions determine whether he is sufficiently righteous to enter Heaven."

Salvation is at root a matter of being united to (or spiritually joined to) the risen Christ. That means the believer is accepted by God because he possesses Christ's own righteousness. Christ *becomes to us* righteousness, sanctification, and redemption, in the words of 1 Corinthians 1:30. But the legalist thinks, "No— I will only be accepted by God if I supplement Christ's righteousness with my own righteousness, a righteousness I accumulate by doing good things." Those good things might include Bible reading, prayer, church attendance, personal devotional times, living with certain lifestyle convictions, or performing Christian service. These are indeed good things that Christians should do! But they do not add to the perfect righteousness that the believer receives from the risen Christ.

Thus legalism is a serious affront to Jesus Christ and the gospel on at least three counts.

First, legalism assaults the Lord Jesus Christ's work on the cross. In particular, legalism undermines the very essence of justification. It requires an unbiblical redefinition of justification, one that could be called "justification by faith in Christ but supplemented by my own works." Legalism says, "I am dissatisfied with my legal standing before God based solely upon Christ's righteousness. That's not good enough. I'm going to add something to what Christ has secured." In maintaining that his righteousness comes (at least in part) by obeying God's laws, the legalist says that Christ died in vain (Galatians 2:21). He may have begun in the Spirit, but he is attempting to attain his goal by human effort (Galatians 3:3).

Second, legalism frustrates grace. How? It promises salvation by technique or formula. J. I. Packer explains:

> Legalism frustrates grace by seeking righteousness through works of law and religion, viewing these as part of our acceptance with God alongside the merits of Christ. But against this Paul insists that faith in Christ for salvation is an exclusive trust, so that a professed trust in Him which does not exclude self-reliance entirely is not real faith in God's sight. Hence Paul's warning to the Judaizing Galatians, who thought they needed to supplement their faith in Christ by being circumcised: "you are severed from Christ, you who would be justified by the law; you have fallen away from grace" (Galatians 5:4). Law-keeping plays no part in justification; justification is by faith alone, because it is in and through Christ alone, and thus it is by grace alone. To trust one's own works alongside the work of Christ dishonors Him, frustrates grace, and cuts one off from life.

Third, legalism robs the Christian of assurance and peace of mind. So long as the believer thinks his standing before God is dependent (even in part) upon his own good works, he can never be certain that he is truly righteous before (and accepted by) God. How does he know if he has done enough good works? Can he be certain that he has prayed enough? Worshiped enough? Witnessed enough? Had enough daily devotional times? How much is *enough*? Assurance that one is accepted before God can *only* come when we are relying wholly upon the perfect righteousness of Jesus Christ. Jesus' imputed righteousness is the only kind of righteousness that is *enough.* As the old hymn writer put it, we dare not trust even the sweetest frame but wholly lean on Jesus' name.

Legalism flourishes where justification by faith alone is misunderstood.

D. But Isn't a Christian Supposed to Do Good Works? Isn't a Christian Supposed to Obey God's Laws?

Absolutely! The Lord Jesus Christ saves people so that they will be zealous for good deeds (Titus 2:14). Disciples are called to be disciplined: "Discipline yourself for the purpose of godliness," writes Paul (1 Timothy 4:7). Denying oneself, taking up one's cross, and following Christ is a mandatory duty, not an optional suggestion (Matthew 16:24). Participating vibrantly in a local church—stimulating one another to holiness, not forsaking our assembling together, encouraging one another—is an obligation for all Christians (Hebrews 10:24-25). The Holy Spirit enables God's people so that the requirements of God's laws are fulfilled in them, not ignored by them (Romans 8:4).

The key is one's attitude regarding the good work. Why is the believer having daily devotional times? What is the motive for giving money to the church? What drives the Christian to pursue personal holiness? The wrong motive is to regard such good works as ways to accumulate one's own righteousness. When the attitude is, "I will earn more grace because I did this thing," doing that thing becomes a kind of bribe. We try to earn or deserve God's blessing with our behavior.

The right motive is gratitude. We work, pray, worship, and serve as a spontaneous expression of our love for God. We cheerfully engage in such good works because we are thankful that we already possess a perfect righteousness. God's free grace in Christ triggers joy in us, a joy that is eager to honor the One whom we love. This makes obedience an act of grateful worship. Question 86 of the Heidelberg Catechism (the joint Reformed-Lutheran catechism written in 1563) states it this way:

> Q. Since, then, we are delivered from our misery by grace alone, through Christ, without any merit of ours, why must we yet do good works?
> A. Because Christ, having redeemed us by His blood, also renews us by His Holy Spirit after His own image, that with our whole life we may show ourselves thankful to God for His benefits, and that He may be praised by us . . . .

"It has been well said," writes J. I. Packer, "that, in the New Testament, doctrine is grace and ethics is gratitude."

The legalist regards obedience as a *condition* for receiving God's grace; the Christian with a proper motive regards obedience as a *response* to God's grace. As the Puritans put it, the godly man works *from* life while the legalist works *for* life.

This truth is worth restating. The Christian does *not* obey God's commands (a) because his acceptance before God is still undecided and what he does (or doesn't do) improves his legal standing before God; (b) in an attempt to earn more of God's love; or (c) to pay back God out of a sense of slavish obligation and thereby lessen his debt to divine grace (or what John Piper calls "the debtor's ethic"). Even the Christian's most virtuous acts are themselves products of God's grace, so the believer cannot earn any merit from them (Ephesians 2:10; 1 Corinthians 15:10; 2 Corinthians 9:8; Romans 15:18). We keep God's commands because the Lord Jesus Christ has *already* redeemed us and has *already* declared us to be righteous before the Father. Obeying God's laws is an act of praise, not a payment.

Theologian John Murray explains: "While it makes void the gospel to introduce works in connection with justification, nevertheless works done in faith, from the motive of love to God, in obedience to the revealed will of God and to the end of His glory, are intrinsically good and acceptable to God. As such they will be the criterion of reward in the life to come."

Legalism often leads to an excessive concern for "religious form" with the unhappy result that "religious substance" is lost, perverted, or otherwise minimized. This means that the legalist might dutifully spend thirty minutes reading his Bible and praying, and yet find such times burdensome, unprofitable, and even painful. This man faithfully puts in his time every morning (that is, he pays attention to religious form) but does not truly worship God nor feed his soul (that is, he neglects religious substance). If the legalist's personal devotions are an attempt to earn righteousness before God—and improve his standing before God—they betray a wrong motive. He is attempting to purchase grace.

I recall my own experience with personal daily devotions as a new Christian. I had been reared a Roman Catholic and was introduced to evangelical Christianity in college. I was biblically illiterate and had scant understanding of justification by faith alone. After my conversion, I was taught to have daily "quiet times" where I read the Bible and prayed. I did this faithfully, and God kindly blessed my reading and praying. As I look back on those days, however, I realize that I went about my quiet times all wrong. When I awoke in the morning, I began my day thinking that I possessed zero righteousness before God. If I had a good quiet time—if I gleaned something from my Bible reading or if I prayed through my prayer list—then I embarked upon my day confident that I was accepted by God. But if I failed to have a good quiet time, I felt unrighteous and believed that I had failed to earn God's grace for that day. Sometimes I would try to have a second quiet time so I could again attempt to establish my righteousness before God.

I realize now that in those early days of my Christian life, I was a Protestant monk. I was legalistically attempting to establish my righteousness on a daily basis by performing my religious duties. I had no sense of waking up in the morning *already* clothed with the perfect righteousness of Christ. Although I thought I understood the concept of justification by faith alone, my understanding of my daily standing before God had nothing to do with Christ's imputed righteousness.

This does *not* mean that we should stop having daily devotional times. A daily quiet time is essential to one's spiritual health and something that you should do if you aren't doing it now. But we must engage in personal devotions from a right motive. Surely we can't treat our quiet times as self-justification sessions where we earn our righteousness before God.

What about church attendance? Is it legalistic to be faithful to local church meetings? It depends upon your motive: why do you do it? Faithfully attending worship services because you love God and long to worship Him is *not* legalistic; going to church in order to earn God's favor or maintain your acceptability before Him *is*.

Some Christians refuse to drink alcoholic beverages. Is this legalism? It depends upon the abstainer's motive. If it is an attempt to earn or "pay back" grace, then that is legalism. If abstinence is either humble obedience to what one believes the Bible to teach or the desire to maintain a good Christian testimony in a community that disapproves of alcohol consumption, then it is not legalistic.

What about wearing certain kinds of clothing? The Scriptures surely call for God's people to dress modestly and decently. No doubt the angels in Heaven weep when so many Christians today dress lasciviously, provocatively, and flirtatiously. Are specific "clothing rules" legalistic? Is it legalistic for women to wear long dresses? Maybe yes, maybe no. It depends on the underlying motive.

Gratitude-driven and joy-triggered law-keeping is good. Misinformed law-keeping may need to be corrected, but it is not necessarily legalism. But if law-keeping is linked to relying upon one's sanctification as one's justification, or if law-keeping is a guilt-ridden "pay back" activity, then it is legalism.

E. What About the Pharisees?

The Pharisees are the poster children for legalism. We see them displaying all kinds of ugly behavior, behavior that elicits Jesus' strongest condemnations. It is important to realize, however, that the Pharisees are never scolded for obeying God's laws too much. Jesus tacitly approves of the Pharisees' careful compliance with the smallest of laws (Luke 11:42) and even condemns them for not obeying God thoroughly enough (Mark 7:8)! The Pharisees' problem was that they obeyed God *from the wrong motives*. The Pharisees saw obedience to God's Word (and things like praying, fasting, and tithing) as a bribe or payment.

Because the Pharisees calculated that their bribes/payments were sufficiently large, they were *self-righteous*. That term literally means they believed their actions made them righteous before God. *Self-justified* is a synonym for *self-righteous*.

This was the focus of Jesus' words in Luke 18:9-14. This parable was aimed specifically at those who "trusted in themselves that they were righteous," which implies that this attitude was especially common among the Pharisees. The parable is also clearly concerned with the issue of justification.

> And He also told this parable to some people who trusted in themselves that they were righteous, and viewed others with contempt: "Two men went up into the temple to pray, one a Pharisee and the other a tax collector. The Pharisee stood and was praying this to himself: 'God, I thank You that I am not like other people: swindlers, unjust, adulterers, or even like this tax collector. I fast twice a week; I pay tithes of all that I get.' But the tax collector, standing some distance away, was even unwilling to lift up his eyes to heaven, but was beating his breast, saying, 'God, be merciful to me, the sinner!' I tell you, this man went to his house justified rather than the other; for everyone who exalts himself will be humbled, but he who humbles himself will be exalted."

Here is legalism unmasked. Ironically, it features an undermining and weakening of God's law. Men who are determined to earn their own righteousness before God soon discover that God's commands are too searching and comprehensive. The best of men find their sin exposed by God's law. This is distressing news for the legalist: how can he justify himself when he repeatedly fails to keep God's commands? The solution is to "dumb down" God's laws: substitute laws we can always keep for the divine laws that we repeatedly break.

Thus the Pharisee in this parable has reduced God's commands to civil decency, ritual fasting, and tithing. This is how he is able to be confident that he is righteous before God: he has fully obeyed what he regards as God's laws. Modern-day legalists do something similar: they substitute their own "easy" laws for God's searching, comprehensive, and sin-exposing laws. God's Ten Commandments, for example, require obedience in thought, deed, and word. Jesus said that we violate the "do not murder" command when we harbor strong feelings of hatred for someone, and we violate the "do not commit adultery" command when we indulge lustful thoughts (Matthew 5:21-22, 27-28). The legalist, however, cannot use these laws to establish his own righteousness because he violates them! Instead, he creates his own checklist (often without realizing what he is doing), one similar to that of the Pharisees: attendance at church meetings, baptism, tithing, doctrinal orthodoxy, no outwardly scandalous conduct, maybe certain standards regarding lifestyle issues.

The result of measuring oneself by such dumbed-down laws is predictable. Like the Pharisee in this parable, we end up thinking that we are justified before God. Like this Pharisee, we give ourselves the credit for allegedly earning this righteousness. (Note the Pharisee's words of self-congratulation: "I fast twice a week, I give tithes of all I get.") Like this Pharisee, we often hold in contempt those who don't keep our laws like we do. This only makes sense: if they tried harder and did what we did, then they, too, could keep the rules. This is why legalism often produces arrogance and self-exaltation ("I'm so glad I did what I did") rather than humility ("God, be merciful to me, the sinner"). This last point is worth emphasizing. Humility, contrition, and brokenness come when we are thoroughly persuaded that we are guilty sinners, men who are poor in spirit before God. This only happens when we measure ourselves against the *real* law of God (and not our dumbed-down version of it). God's laws reveal to us that even our best works are tainted by sin.

Sinful men are devilishly creative when it comes to "taming" or easing the demands of God's law. Here are several popular techniques:

- Focus upon the outward form of God's command while neglecting the spiritual substance of devotion to God. Attend church but don't attend unto the worship of God and the building up of the saints. Remain faithfully married to your spouse but neglect to love him/her biblically. In Matthew 23:16-24, Jesus describes this as neglecting the weightier matters of God's law.
- Restrict God's commands to outward behavior and ignore His concern with motives and attitudes. Murder no one but permit anger and rage to fester within you. Never commit outward adultery but secretly feed and indulge lust in your heart. This is a negation of what Christians have traditionally called "the spirituality of the law," or the realization that God's laws always reach past external behavior to internal attitudes.
- Privilege manmade religious rules (or applications) so that they override or replace God's laws (Matt. 15:3-9, Mark 2:16-3:6, 7:1-8).
- Reject Old Testament moral laws as inapplicable today. Charles Haddon Spurgeon rightly corrects this thinking: "No child of God seeks for any dispensation to exempt him from any of his Master's commands."

One especially insidious technique for enfeebling God's laws is to portray holiness primarily or substantially as not doing certain things. Holiness surely includes not doing specific sins, but it includes much more than that. It includes positive conformity to the very highest kind of moral purity. Indeed, holiness is (at root) conformity to the moral image of the Lord Jesus Christ. The Messiah both abstained from specific unrighteous behaviors and continuously performed righteous ones. Legalism seems especially attractive in settings where holiness is portrayed almost exclusively in terms of what we don't do. J. I. Packer expresses this well in his explanation of how the Puritans understood sanctification. "Puritan ethical teaching took the form of a positive ideal of zealous and wise godliness, at which Christians must always be aiming even though they never fully reach it in this world," writes Packer. "And unattained positive ideals are the death of the legalistic spirit, which can only flourish in an atmosphere of negative restriction where abstinence is regarded as the essence of virtue." (*A Quest for Godliness: The Puritan Vision of the Christian Life*, p. 119) Packer's point: legalism dies when the full demands of God's law—including positive godly behaviors—are made clear.

F. Can a Justified Person Displease God?

Yes. A Christian can be simultaneously righteous before God and displeasing to God.

The Bible frequently uses a father-son paradigm to explain how God deals with His people. The oft-used phrase *child of God* attests to this, as do (a) God's own characterizing of Himself as the *Father* of His people, (b) the doctrine of adoption, and (c) specific passages like Luke 15:11-32 and Hebrews 12:3-11. This father-son paradigm is also helpful in understanding how secure and eternally-loved children of God can nonetheless displease their heavenly Father.

Consider my own son. No matter what happens, he will always be a member of the Spinney family. I love him with a love that is unconditional and irrevocable. Especially when I think of *love* as *covenant faithfulness and commitment*, I can never love him *any more* than I do now nor *any less* than I do now. Sad to say, however, my son can disobey me and thereby displease me. He can verify that displeasing Dad often results in pain, tears, and loss. But such displeasure never jeopardizes our permanent father-son relationship or my son's permanent status as a family member. Such displeasure often triggers correction and discipline, but not a termination of our relationship. By the same token, my son doesn't purchase my love or win my fatherly commitment to him by pleasing me.

Should my son obey me and thereby please me? Absolutely! My son should be motivated to obey me by a desire to express love and gratitude toward me— not a desperate fear that I will disown him if he isn't obedient enough (Romans 8:15). And at those times when my young son doesn't feel like pleasing his dad with obedience, he hopefully will trust me and operate on the assumption that obedience to my commands is in his best interest.

A justified saint displeases God by sinning. However, sinning doesn't make him unjustified or less justified . . . for the simple reason that *not* sinning (i.e., obeying) did not make him justified in the first place. The Christian's righteousness is a gift received, not a status earned (Romans 5:16-17).

G. How Long Will the War Against Legalism Last?

It would be nice if all vestiges of self-righteousness were eradicated from Christians the moment they were regenerated. If believers entered the Christian life with a full and undistorted understanding of justification by faith alone through grace alone in Christ alone, perhaps they would not struggle with legalism. But that's not what happens. The believer's sin penalty is paid and sin's power is broken, but sin's remnants remain to be battled. Thankfully, saints do not battle alone. As the Holy Spirit renews their minds through the Word of God, they are enabled by His power to put to death the deeds of the body and bear the peaceable fruit of righteousness. One of these deeds of the body is *self-righteousness*, and the fruit of the Spirit includes humility. For the entirety of his earthly sojourn, the believer will see lingering vestiges of self-righteousness in himself and will be called to crucify them. More and more, the growing Christian will learn to rest wholly in the imputed righteousness of the risen Christ.

Thus the fight against legalism is one in which every Christian participates. The opening battle was won when the Holy Spirit exposed the sinner's failure to keep God's laws, worked repentance in him, and enabled him to trust Christ for salvation. That was the first time that the saint renounced his own righteousness as his legal basis for standing before God; that was the first time that he instead threw himself upon the alien righteousness of Jesus Christ. But the saint continually fights against legalistic thinking as he matures in Christ. Sanctification means he appreciates more fully the comprehensive demands of God's laws, the poverty of his own righteousness, and the sufficiency of the Christ-supplied righteousness that he receives in justification. Sanctification means he is weaned more and more from the vestiges of self-righteousness while relying more and more on the provision of Christ's righteousness.

Oh, that we could repudiate legalism once and for all and be rid of it forever! But repudiating legalism is like repudiating selfishness, impatience, idolatry, and unkindness. Sanctification involves a lifetime of repudiating such things.

The Remedy for Legalism

The ultimate remedy for legalism is the same remedy for many problems in the Christian life: appreciate more fully the Lord Jesus Christ and what He accomplished at Calvary.

I recall the day that a Jehovah's Witness came to my home. He presented a Watchtower monologue; I sat and listened. When it was my turn to talk, I said, "We disagree over what happened when Jesus Christ died on the cross." He seemed surprised by my words. I continued: "There are only two possible ways of understanding what happened at Calvary. I'll set them before you, and you choose the one you think is true." He listened curiously so I continued.

"Do you believe this: that when Jesus died on the cross, He made it *possible* for you to be approved by God, provided that you do your part? Do you think that Jesus accomplished perhaps ninety-five percent of the task of making you righteous before God, but that now the ball is in your court? Do you think that now you must do your part— now you need to add to what Christ did so that God will accept you? Will your own good works now make you righteous before God, and will your refusal to do enough good works make you unacceptable before God? Is that what you think happened?

"Or do you think Jesus' death on the cross secured and guaranteed your approval before God? Do you think that the Lord Jesus Christ fully accomplished all there is to accomplish regarding your acceptance by God? Do you think God's Son did one hundred percent of the work in making you righteous before God? Do you think Jesus secured all the grace, love, and righteousness there is to secure, and now gives it all to you as a free gift?"

When I laid out these two options, the Jehovah's Witness didn't hesitate for a moment. He said, "I believe in the first scenario. Of course I have to do my part."

Most Bible-believing Christians will see this man's response for what it is: a bold affirmation of "works salvation" and a nullification of the gospel of grace. This was high octane legalism, a legalism that intentionally brought good works into the matter of justification.

But it's not just Jehovah's Witnesses that believe this. I suspect that many in conservative salvation-by-grace-alone churches believe this as well— not as crassly or as openly as this Jehovah's Witness, but they still believe it. They may not even fully realize that they believe it. They may affirm that they are saved by faith alone; in reality, they are relying partly upon their sanctification to make a contribution to their justification.

"We all automatically gravitate toward the assumption that we are justified by our level of sanctification," writes Richard Lovelace, "and when this posture is adopted it inevitably focuses our attention not on Christ but on the adequacy of our own obedience. We start each day with our personal security resting not on the accepting love of God and the sacrifice of Christ but on our present feelings or recent achievements in the Christian life." Then Lovelace adds this illuminating observation: "Since these arguments will not quiet the human conscience, we are inevitably moved either to discouragement and apathy or to a self-righteousness which falsifies the record to achieve a sense of peace."

What is true for the Jehovah's Witness is true for you: the Lord Jesus Christ's obedience is the sole basis for the sinner's acceptance by God. What could be more complete than the perfect righteousness—earned painstakingly by the Son of God over an entire human lifetime—that culminated in His death on the cross? Can you imagine how high Jesus' "holiness score" was? It was off the chart; in fact, it was perfect. And when Jesus died on the cross, God made Him who knew no sin to be sin on our behalf—our sin was transferred to Him in such a manner that He effectually became sin personified—that we might become the righteousness of God by virtue of our saving union with Christ (2 Corinthians 5:21). Just as sin was transferred to the Messiah, so His perfect righteousness was transferred to us. So when God's people stand before the Father, they have Jesus' perfect righteousness as their own "holiness score."

And now I'm going to do *my part*? I'm going to add to Jesus' perfect righteousness? My quiet time will make me more acceptable to God? My church attendance will earn me more grace? Perish the arrogant thought that the feeble works of a sinful man can supplement what Christ did on the cross!

If I truly understand what Jesus did at Calvary, I'll never try to add anything to what He accomplished.

If I truly understand what Jesus did at Calvary, I will come boldly to the throne of grace. I will approach the thrice holy God with full confidence that He accepts me— not because I had a good day but because I have a great Savior.

If I truly understand what Jesus did at Calvary, I will understand that on my worst day, I'm *still* clothed in the righteousness of Christ and therefore am *still* accepted in the Beloved.

If I truly understand what Jesus did at Calvary, my joy will overflow— so much so that I will express it by obeying Christ. Love for Christ and joyful gratitude will supply a far stronger motive for obedience than the desire to earn grace or somehow pay back God. I will present my body as a living sacrifice to God. I'll say with the old hymn writer Isaac Watts, "Love so amazing, so divine, demands my soul, my life, my all."

OTHER TITLES FROM TULIP BOOKS

HOW TO SURVIVE YOUR PASTOR'S SERMONS: Six Ways to Make Pulpit Messages More Profitable to Your Soul

WHY DO BAD THINGS HAPPEN TO GOOD PEOPLE? Thinking Biblically About the Problem of Sin in Our World

PEEKING INTO THE DEVIL'S PLAYBOOK: Satan's Strategies for Tempting Christians to Sin

DID GOD CREATE SPORTS ALSO? Thinking Christianly About Sports

LOOKING FOR GOD IN ALL THE WRONG PLACES: An Appeal for Word-Based Corporate Worship

DRESSED TO KILL: Thinking Biblically About Modest and Immodest Clothing

WHAT IS THE MEANING OF BAPTISM? A Guide For Christians Preparing For Baptism

MONKEYING AROUND WITH DANGEROUS IDEAS: Four Reasons Outside the Field of Science Why Christians Should Reject Evolutionary Thinking